Bread Machine Mastery

Bread Machine Mastery

Harper Northwood

Contents

1

Introduction

This book is an in-depth guide to several elements of mastering crafting artisan breads by using a bread machine. Readers will obtain an understanding of how and why most artisan breads are prepared and baked, leading to a deeper understanding and mastery of it. Learners will also become familiar with several stages of the artisan breadmaking process and techniques, which can be used with many bread machines. The use of time and hands are two critical byproducts of the bread machine's prevalence in today's households, and this tool is commonly used for its expressiveness as a result. Thus, these three detailed elements, often overlooked by lengthy manuals, are addressed: rest and rise time, the tricky hands divergence, and the range of texture and flavor-related options for the bread's various stages. Below is an outline that guides you through the next 13 pages.

Bread Machine Basics and Techniques: Artisan Baking ABCDEF Introduction Why Hostess, Entrepreneurs, or the Relaxed Bakers of Today Love Bread Machines. The Slow and the Fast: What a Bread Maker Can Do for You and Why Its Function Matters to You A Preview of Mastery: The Six Arts of Artisan Baking that You Can Learn from a Bread Machine

About Bread Machines

Once upon a time, the bread-making process took up several hours a day, every day. Now, modern homemakers can skip all the work and leave day-long sourdoughs to those artisan bakeries on the corner. If you do still want to bake bread fresh at home, you can snag a bread machine to do the hard work for you. Bread machines are electric appliances that mix, ferment, and bake bread. You put all the ingredients in, and the machine heats them up to the right temperature to help the bread rise. It kneads the dough, then lets it sit so the yeast can do its work. Finally, the machine bakes the loaf. These machines can bake a variety of truly delicious breads, from a basic white loaf to a hearty whole grain. Gluten-free, low-sugar, and quick-bake breads are possible, too. Bread machines tend to be shaped like a box with an interior pan to hold the dough. They have a few buttons and a digital display to help you select the right baking program.

Using a bread machine, a home baker can make artisan breads that meet the approval of any master baker. If you happen to be curious about or interested in making sourdough bread but are hesitant to tackle the more labor-intensive process, you will learn how simple "sourdoughing" can be. The ease of bread-machine bread will surprise you. There is an authentic feel to the changing of textures, the gradual change before your eyes. The satisfaction is indescribably rewarding for anyone who savors delicious bread fresh from the oven. In bread-machine baking, you may choose to let the machine do the mixing, kneading, rising, punching, and an occasional resting while choosing to shape or bake an oven-roasting loaf. Following are easy as 1-2-3 directions for artisan bread baking in a bread machine.

Benefits of Baking Bread at Home

Bread is one of the oldest and most loved staples in the world, though more and more people are discovering and rediscovering the value of creating these hearty grains in a home environment. People have baked bread for thousands of years, long before the conveniences of modern appliances and supermarkets, so people do not need bread makers to produce loaves of their own. Still, bread machines offer people many advantages. They save time and physical labor, make baking less intimidating, and ensure professional results.

Nonetheless, there are potential downsides to bread machines. Customers should think about the pros and cons and the likely best fit for their lifestyle when considering whether to purchase and use a bread machine. Companies have perfected countless models with different features to help this process. The bread will always contain basic yeast, flour, salt, and water regardless of the bread machine that you have, something that is hard to replicate in the commercial market that favors long shelf lives and discreet flavors. But that does not mean people can't choose spices, flavorings, dried fruits, nuts, or even wine and cheese. When people make their bread, they escape from many other issues, such as unhealthy, extra fat and additives, cleanliness issues, or allergies.

2

Understanding Bread Machines

As we gear up to make beautiful loaves of bread, let's take some time to build a comprehensive understanding of bread machines. We will start with a brief history of bread machines and move into how the machines are constructed and their basic operating principles from there. To establish a certain amount of common ground and understanding, we will go through the two components of bread making that the bread machine breaks into steps. We will also tackle the most common misconceptions about how and why the bread machine works the way it does.

Bread machines were released into the consumer market in 1987. Over the years, companies began refining the designs and adding some new features and conveniences. In the last 10 years or so, machines have not changed much at all. In other words, if you purchased a middle-of-the-line bread machine today, it will virtually work the same as it did 20 odd years ago. You have to look past flashier sales tactics to make a decision. Every bread machine, regardless of its brand, design, and so on, contains three basic elements: a small AC synchronous motor; a baffled mixing and baking pan; and an electrical control circuit. We will cover all of these components in far more detail later, but for now, it is very important for you to have a very general understanding of these three components and their primary roles.

Types of Bread Machines

Bread machines of all types are made to make bread and other products using the same step-by-step process, including mixing, resting, kneading, proofing, and finally baking. We here will explain each different bread machine type as below:

Single Loaf Bread Machines: Single loaf bread machines contain only one bread pan and one kneading blade. The loaf size that these machines produce varies widely from 1 to 2.5 pounds, with a variety of size options in between. Virtually all bread machines with only one pan available in the United States produce a horizontal loaf with a standard 4×8" or 5×9" bread pan. The two largest single loaf bread machines, in addition to the horizontal pans, also have vertical loaf pans available.

Dual Loaf Bread Machines: In contrast to the single loaf bread machines, every dual loaf bread machine contains two kneading blades and two bread pans. Just like their single loaf counterparts, the sizes of the loaves available vary from one machine to another, as well as the shapes of the loaf pans. An option for having both pans be horizontal pans as well as both vertical is available, as well as models with a horizontal loaf in a 5×8.25" loaf pan and a vertical in a 4" loaf pan or a horizontal loaf in a 4×5/8" pan and a vertical in a 4×4" loaf pan. One thing that really has set the dual loaf bread machines apart is the "dual settings," which allow each of the loaves to be completely different from one another.

Key Features and Functions

The most important features you'll want to consider when choosing a machine for creating artisan bread are the bowls, paddles, proofing settings, and custom or manual settings.

Length Inside Bread Barrel. Select the bread machine which has the longest bread barrel. The right size plays a very important role in making good bread. The barrel whose length is as long as 208 mm, width is 135 mm, and depth is 180 mm is very suitable for a family. The bread is in nice shape after baking and has as many as 500 grams. Again, a larger machine size is necessary for making larger loaves. Single or Double! The bread machine produces a larger loaf and hence they need machines baking. In some machines, baking has options and you can switch from one to the other if you like (it's all for making and is not easy). Some of the producers of the bread machine, such as Cuisinart, produce a smaller machine that also has a sandwich tank in the top. The yeast dispenser – you didn't know you wanted to use this feature. The yeast dispenser shouldn't be the reason you choose a machine; nevertheless, they can be really handy. The biggest advantage is the ability to add high acid elements (like fruits or cheese) later on in the kneading stage which would adversely affect the rising action of the yeast. In some machines, this is conjoined with raisin bread mode.

3

Essential Ingredients for Artisan Breads

Creating bread in a bread machine can be a simple and easy task, and more than that, it can be a flavorful and aesthetically pleasing task as well. Being able to ask merely a few ingredients in your machine and have it return you a beautiful and crusty loaf of your choosing is always an enjoyable experience. Whether you are making bread to accompany dinner, design the perfect sandwich, or just to be able to toast up buttery crisps in the morning, creating a uniquely flavored bread changes the game. When we make bread in the machine, we focus on the basic, essential ingredients to allow the machine to activate the yeast and ferment the dough. Below you will find a list of the most crucial ingredients in making bread. Alternatives and other recommendations follow the TS Bordeaux recipe with similar ingredients elsewhere in this blog.

The most basic and essential aspect of baking bread is to include flour, water, salt, and yeast. These four ingredients work together to create a crust and crumb that is so desirable in the bread baking community. While we mainly stick to creating doughs with these four ingredients, exceptions always dabble in here and there to create unique loaves. Different flours will allow for not only different flavors but also different gluten structures as well. Water activates the fermentation process. When combined with flour and yeast, it activates a fermenting process that will eventually create the bread. Salt adds flavor to your dough as well, but it also serves as a retarding ingredient in bread dough. Salt regulates the fermentation process by letting the machine stop the ferment when adding all your ingredients, which we will talk about more later. Salt also strengthens our dough by reducing the gas that is produced by yeast. In turn, that allows our dough to rise. Yeast will activate and let your dough rise. Yeast breaks down the sugars, creating alcohol and carbon dioxide, which allow the dough to rise. The alcohol will then evaporate in the oven.

Flour Selection

While one of the key appeals of a bread machine is its "dump and go" capabilities, the quality of the flour used is a very important consideration. Should you use bread flour or all-purpose flour, or the combination of these two that is often found in bread machine recipes? Should you select organic flour milled from hard white-wheat berries, whole grain flour, whole wheat flour (which has a coarser texture), or pastry flour, the softest of the flours and typically unsuitable for rustic breads? These variables are all instrumental to the development of protein. As proteins begin to absorb water, they form chains of amino acids, which create the structure for the gluten, the key nonlinear protein that creates a certain chewiness of the bread. A good first rule to follow in flour choice is to start with flour that has a higher protein content. Any of the milled or artisan flours being sold for use in bread machines are more than likely good choices. In the past few years, some of the prices of artisan flours from smaller mills have become more competitive with the well-branded commercially milled flours.

I worked with Peter Lor Nielsen, a Danish baker, who suggested that whoever stops the starch granule on its way to 160° will get a much better flavor. This, of course, takes time. Time is what flour wants. Time is what makes the kind of fermentation we have been talking about possible. Time is closely related to temperature. With the combination of time and temperature, delicate flavors are produced. The crumb of your bread is influenced in this same lingering way, by the temperature at which it was baked. Formulas from tagier, a French bread-baking magazine that I edited, read like thermal maps; they state the temperature you would use to strike the precise tone of flavor in your bread. Uniform ovens turn the bread-outing process into a clean musical score that anybody can play. If you bake your bread at a high uniform temperature, under the regulating supervision of a good bread machine, the crumb and crust that you so artfully baked by nursing your dough for hours in your artisan wicker baskets will taste one note worse than mass-produced bread from the corner supermarket. Uniform ovens are there to make biscuits. Crusty artisanal breads beg for the accents of natural ovens.

Yeast and Leavening Agents

Leavening agents are one of the most important elements in the bread-making process. They help the bread rise by creating bubbles from carbon dioxide. Consequently, the texture of the bread becomes lighter, more porous, and chewier. The increased air or gas in the dough also acts to inflate the bread. The result is a lighter and softer finished product that has the volume to carry the flavor of the bread throughout every bite. Yeast, whether instant, active dry, bread machine or cake, and chemical leaveners like baking powder and baking soda, are leavening agents that are employed for raising bread.

Yeast Basics: Experiments, in general, show that the most satisfactory results are obtained with either active dry yeast or instant yeast in bread-machine baking. Cake yeast may be used in bread machines converted for the purpose, but the results were far less satisfactory. Conversion is necessary for cake yeast and may vary by manufacturer; therefore, please refer to each individual bread machine's instruction book for additional information. There are several types of commercially available yeasts, all of which have a characteristic difference in moisture content and size. When purchasing yeast for bread-machine baking, look for the type of yeast specified in the recipe. It is important to follow the manufacturer's suggestions or those provided with the bake mode settings in the recipe, as different types of yeast have different proofing and work best at different times and with different bread-making cycles. Baking with unconditioned yeast will result in failure of the recipe and poor-quality bread. Yeast is a plant-type cell that helps bread dough rise. Yeast is utilized as a leavening agent in breads. Do not combine yeast with salt in the dough-making process. Yeast can be producing dead cells and can also dissolve the salt. Yeast is a fungus that is made up of individual strands, similar to chains of sausage links. Yeast should never come into direct contact with salt when bread dough is being mixed. Combining yeast and salt can kill the yeast cells, which can cause bread dough to fall. Yeast is considerably larger than salt granules, and the two ingredients may be craftily combined beneath the surface of the dough. Follow the recipe's instructions and always add the yeast first before layering the salt on top.

4

Mastering Basic Bread Recipes

From sourdough to whole grain to rustic loaves, every homemade artisan bread starts with a straightforward and easy-to-master basic dough. To give you the bread design you've been craving, there are just a few basic bread recipes you need to become comfortable with. The bread machine steps up and does the work of kneading and proving, yielding a dough that is a pleasure to work with. Other recipes will require mixing, kneading, and proofing dough by hand. However, a practice run through four kinds of basic bread machine loaves will show you what doughs at their many stages should look and feel like. When you move onto more complicated bread types, this base knowledge will be really helpful to have.

Simple white bread is the easiest yeast bread to make. It is one of the most common types of yeast bread, only requiring five key ingredients: yeast, flour, butter, sugar, and salt. Thanks to its simple procedures, the bread machine and bread recipes are both fantastic educational guides. If you haven't tried rye bread before, perhaps you should. Rye bread has a distinctly earthy, slightly nutty flavor that pairs well with white or wheat bread. And, since rye flour doesn't have as much gluten as wheat, the crumb is also a little more intense. Whole wheat bread is made white bread with half of the white flour replaced with whole wheat, resulting in a classic, lighter whole wheat sandwich bread. The flavor of 100 percent whole wheat can be craved by more nostalgic eaters and those interested in whole foods. It is the most difficult of the basic bread recipes for a bread machine to make well. After the first rising, the dough will be formable, but it may not seem particularly soft and smooth. In the bread machine, don't overknead. For the best taste, whole grain bread will also need to use the right sweetening.

White Bread

White bread is often simple and straightforward. While there are as many variations as there are bread bakers, certain features are shared. Bakers make a mixture of bread flour (for its higher protein quantity) and all-purpose flour to achieve a mix that is neither too dense nor too light. Perfecting a white bread loaf is a lesson in understanding how yeast works and what best influences its activation. Through understanding the basics of operating a bread machine, making white bread at home becomes an achievable task.

The first thing you should keep in mind, after reviewing what you have and what you need, is the temperature of your ingredients. Maintaining proper ingredient temperature not only speeds things up, but it creates a more humid dough overall that proves in less time and tastes better by extracting more flavor from the yeast and creating an even stronger gluten network in the process. Since everything's cool, except for the room itself, err on the side of warmth. Warm water helps the dough rise faster, particularly in a bread machine bowl that can't trap much external warmth at all. Concentrate on 70°F (21°C). A bit warmer usually is fine, up to and including 90°F (32°C). Be cautious with the yeast, however. Overwarmth can "kill" the yeast entirely, so don't have the temperature exceed 138°F

(59°C). If you drop the yeast into some lukewarm water, it will activate without difficulty. Many bitters, including the bitter bretts, don't do anything for a minute to three minutes, but then grow. The water should look creamy and bubbling, with noticeable expansion from overtly activated yeast along the top of the "rise" when activation occurs. If it happens but takes longer than three minutes, assign two to three shakes of yeast, avoid the wort for at least five minutes, and try again.

Whole Wheat Bread

The first thing that you want to consider is which kind of bread that you have in mind that you want to make. Bread comes in many different forms: whole wheat, potato, white, rye, and even sweet breads. Take your time and figure out which ones are on the top of your to-do list, and then make your shopping list and get to it.

Whole Wheat Bread is perhaps the tastiest of the healthy bread picks. Being a fan of whole grain and multigrain breads, I would have to say that making Whole Wheat bread in my bread machine is my favorite, and the recipe has never failed me. When you bake a loaf of Whole Wheat bread in the machine, it is denser and heavier than when a white bread is baked. This is a great result of baking with whole wheat flour. When eating a loaf of bread that has been made with whole wheat flour, it gives you a great feeling of satisfaction knowing that it is dense and wholesome, and will go a long way in letting the hungry feeling subside. Wheat flour will give a loaf of bread structure, wire and a good mouth-feel that is able to stand up as the perfect carrier for two thick layers of your favorite sandwich ingredients. There are many people out there that do not bake with whole wheat flour simply because they think that it will be heavy and dense. It is true that there are a few tricks and tips to having a nice, high quality loaf of bread coming out of the machine.

5

Exploring Artisan Bread Varieties

There are quite a few artisan breads ready for you to explore, hundreds if you venture further into the unknown end of bread crafting. If you have used your bread machine primarily for dough making, you may have been reluctant to explore what's available when it comes to using the entire baking cycle of your machine. Here we have 5 bread machine recipes to give a try. These recipes are a step outside of the normal bread fare that you might expect.

European bread, often called French or Vienna, has a large crust and an inconsistent, irregular crumb texture with visible voids. Artisan European bread has batter consistency pre-baking and that is how you will find ours as well. We give no measurements on flour or water; these will be added a bit at a time at the end of preparation. Our recipe is made using a bread machine to complete the dough and give it the chance to rise in a consistent environment. We then bake off the loaves in a brick oven on a stone hearth. To bake at home, heat the oven to 375 and spray the finished dough loaf with water and cover it with foil to trap the steam. Bake for about half an hour, until golden brown, then slash the top to release steam and bake for another ten minutes. We usually double this recipe and complete it in two batches because our bread machine can only handle about 7 cups of flour at a time.

Sourdough

Once you've made a loaf or two or ten of the white or honey-wheat or oatmeal bread and are comfortable with the functioning of your bread machine, it is time to expand your repertoire to include the artisan breads that are beloved. Let's start with the healthful, rustic bread labeled as "sourdough," though it's completely possible to make a sourdough without any sourness at all! Real sourdough is comprised of wheat flour, water, and salt. However, we are using a Sour Alaskan Sourdough Bread mix that includes a flavor of rye flour and a hint of malt, among the ingredients. The use of white or clear flour brings a lighter, fragrant aspect to our denser breads, which are still packed with nutrients.

While some bakers use bread flour or a purchased starter for bread-machine sourdough, we strongly recommend using the provided San Francisco Sourdough starter culture along with the clay baker method for the closest taste and texture to what our testers are enjoying with our bread-making process. Bread-machine sourdough can be tricky outside of the facilities of a bread-making company. It is important to know that the clay baker slightly caramelizes the outside of the bread resulting in a darker-colored, crunchy, creamy crust and has provided excellent review for our tests. If you do want to give it a try, we suggest waiting until you've felt secure enough baking within your bread machine and a clay baker or cooking bag before you change the recipe given. Starting with the brown-rice flour lining and kneading in the machine but shaping, rising, and baking the bread in the clay baker or bag may be a smooth transitional adjustment to make, or you may wish to change other aspects of the recipe as preferred. It is certainly simple.

6

Advanced Techniques for Artisan Baking

Once a beginner has become comfortable using a bread machine and with the basic process of baking a standard loaf of bread, the more complex and artisanal styles can be approached. For those just learning, artisan bread techniques can be excellent fundamentals for mastering other, more advanced bread machine recipes. The Artisan Bread will further introduce and expand on the concepts that were introduced in previous sections, from pre-ferments to more advanced shaping and scoring concepts. Since the method of developing gluten naturally through a wet, pre-fermented dough was already introduced, the pan method for making yeast bread will first be introduced before the basic sourdough techniques.

The science and methods of artisan—aka hand-crafted—breads are not known well to most of the American public. With the invention of the bread machines, most people now have the wonderful capability to make these kinds of bread at home, with ease and minimal risk. The reason for the appeal of the term "artisan" baking is twofold. First, it sounds exotic and opulent. Anything that sounds refined is automatically connected with wealth in a capitalistic society. Next, the breads created with it seal gourmet images in our rate and as yet un-iced decorated cake with the words "Happy Birthday Young Frank" within the available space, and did it with such perfect confidence that it never occurred to the viewer to suspect it as anything other than handsome planning which, coincidentally, sang. So don't assume that you can score only peasant squiggles on a country boule.

When considering a decor in which a design can be imposed between cuts in the dough or even added to the surrounding design, bear in mind that the visual center of a bread made this way is the center of the design rather than the center of the loaf. If the very center of the loaf is more interesting or easier for slicing and placement, you may well need to adjust the decor so as to avoid attracting undue attention to an unattractive or prosy part of the loaf. The decoction should appear related. Traditionally in French decor, the score lines are doubled, with one running parallel just above the other. This has practical and esthetic value as it makes the design, which will in time disappear, more durable as well as more clear.

7

Troubleshooting Common Bread Machine Issues

There are common issues that may come up when using your bread machine to make artisan bread. Knowing the signs and solutions presented here can mean the difference between a golden brown, fresh loaf of homemade bread and a flat, sour heap of crumbs that just wasted an afternoon in the kitchen.

Crust is more brown than desired: The crust of the bread loaf gets its color from a chemical reaction called the Maillard reaction, the same that makes meat turn brown and flavorful when browned in the skillet. If the crust tends to get burned, try these tricks: Add more sweetener - sugar, honey or agave syrup will cause the equivalent of caramelization to happen, and this can occur at lower temperatures than the Maillard reaction. Lastly, if your bread is done on top before it's done on the bottom, the solution is to cover the bread in the oven with a layer of foil about 2/3 of the way through baking.

Bread is not baking properly: If you're getting a liquid consistency in the center, don't throw out that bread - mix in flour a tablespoon at a time until it forms a ball of dough, then shape back into a loaf and let rise again for 30 minutes. This time, increase the length of the second rise to two hours. If most of the ingredients are liquid, pull the dough out just as this phase ends and before the bread machine starts kneading, wipe off the paddles on the underside of the loaf, and remove the bucket from the oven, wiping the dough away from the sides of the bucket before returning it for baking.

Overproofing

When we degas our dough, either as per the recipes or to keep from having to mess with it too much when we get it out after it makes, we're kind of forcing the dough to proof a bit more. Consequently, the second rise tends to go a bit faster than when you take your bread out of the machine after you've programmed it. To slow down this second rise, hold in moisture, and keep an even texture throughout the bread, you might want to wrap it in your dough cycle with plastic and put it in the fridge for a little while. This can really help with texture and getting a sweeter crumb and better flavor.

Overproofing is a catch-all term for degassed dough, and it happens when you leave your bread in the machine, either with or without the bread making cycle, for more than 20 minutes in a normal environment (by that, I mean a climate reasonably free of vapors and a room temperature of somewhere around 68-70 degrees). It can also happen if the temperature of the room is 80-85 degrees at an equivalent humidity level. Some machines (usually ones with a "keep warm" cycle) can make fairly decent bread this way, whereas others just produce doorstops. If your machine can handle proofing nicely (like the Zo), then you can test to see if your dough is overproofed with the old Two Finger Test, which we'll discuss later in the Bread Basics section. It isn't used often with the Bread Machine Roast and Please, I'd Love Some More doughs because they may never really rise to the point that your finger makes marks in the dough. If, on the other hand, you have a bread maker that rises well, then you'll know right off if your bread is approaching the proof mark and pop it out if you want to shorten this step a bit.

Uneven Baking

1. Flour in pan. 2. Aged ingredients. 3. Pouring hole. 4. Salt.

Uneven baking is caused by several different factors. Uneven temperatures are caused when the flour becomes packed down on one side of the pan. If you store flour in a canister or large jar and refill your flour container from there, you pack fresh flour into the top of the canister. Thus, the top third of the canister or jar has old flour in it and the bottom has fresh flour. Flour becomes packed after about 2 weeks of packing it. Thus, over time, the flour in the bottom becomes packed down, which causes the bread to bake darker on the sides touching this spot, whereas the high poured side is not as dark. The easiest solution is to pour the flour from this container into a bowl, whisk the flour in the bowl to aerate, then re-scoop into the measuring cup and continue as usual.

Excess bread found on the engine will result in uneven baking. If this happens, always take out the pan by using 2 pot holders or oven mitts, turn off and unplug the bread machine, carefully remove the baked bread, and using a hot pad or pot holder, brush off the flour from the side. After the pan and 1 kneading blade are put back in the machine, take the remaining dough and put it back in the pan. A small rising will occur and then it will bake a rounder loaf. Baking will not change, as very little time was lost in the first half of the bake cycle. If you forget to turn off the machine and unplug it, no worries, just finish out the cycle. As soon as the baking is done, remove the pan and using pot holders and a hot pad, brush off flour and bake the remaining dough in the oven.

8

Maintaining and Cleaning Your Bread Machine

Whether you use your bread machine seldom or every day, it has to be cleaned and maintained in order to prolong its life. Always switch off or unplug your bread machine and allow it to cool down first before performing any type of cleaning or maintenance.

Unplug the power cord and let the unit cool down before removing any parts or performing any cleaning. When you have let the unit cool, remove the bread pan and the kneading blade. Use a soft cloth or a sponge to wipe the inside of the bread machine with a mild liquid detergent, then set the bread machine on its side to dry out. Use a mild cloth or sponge moistened with a light soapy solution to wash the bread pan and kneading blade. Use a non-metallic brush to clean the knuckle. Wash the inside and outside of the lid. If you are using soap or detergent, make sure it is free of microbeads. Also, avoid using abrasives, such as steel wool or harsh household cleaners, which will mar the surfaces. Rinse the parts with warm water and let them air dry. Wipe the surface of the bread machine with a gentle cloth. Never immerse the bread machine in water or pour water onto it. The bread pan and kneading blade are not safe to use in the dishwasher. Allow the bread machine to dry thoroughly before reassembling it and using it again.

If necessary, thoroughly dry the bread pan and kneading blade. Periodically wash out the bread pan and kneading blade. Soak the bread pan in hot, soapy water if you have food that is stuck in it. Make sure the knuckle is thoroughly dried with a clean tea towel before placing the blade into your bread pan. Lubricate the bread pan's knuckle according to the manufacturer's instructions. Ensure the kneading blade is fitted to the bread pan correctly by pushing down the kneading shaft so that it clicks into place. Regularly check that the kneading blade is securely in position before your loaf is loaded into the bread machine. Let the bread pan's knuckle cool down after you remove it from the bread machine and before washing it up.

9

Baking Bread with Alternative Ingredients

Reading through this entire guide in one sitting, readers might get the impression that to bake an artisan bread, one either uses white flour or a mixture of white and whole-wheat flour. However, you can actually bake up to four dozen varieties of specialty breads made from unique ingredients or a blend of ingredients. These ingredients include white flour (about 80% of the flour mixture), whole-wheat flour, corn flour, sugared infused fruits and vegetables, cornmeal, mashed potatoes or sweet potatoes or yams, rolled oats, mashed beans, textured vegetable proteins, wheat gluten, malt, malt syrup, barley soup, soy flour, peanut flour, rice flour, shredded coconut, cream of coconut, vegetable or olive oils, seeds of your choice such as sunflower seeds, pumpkin seeds, chia seeds, and poppy seeds, and a little pinch of spices such as nutmeg, cinnamon, cocoa powder, pepper, or Southwest spices. Experiment with a teaspoon or a tablespoon of an ingredient or a mixture of two or three ingredients; then expect to bake a variety of specialty breads to suit your palate. You will find a few examples of artisan bread recipes that use either two cups of mashed vegetables, a 15-ounce can of beans, or both, as well as 1-3 tablespoons of spices that include garlic or a blend of basil, oregano, thyme, or paprika sprinkled in the midst of baking two loaves from the wet-ingredient cycle.

If you want to explore baking additional varieties of these alternative breads, then you will bake enough of these alternative breads to provide and offer samples of your baking progress. Most people are fascinated with the aroma of fresh-baked bread and will be your taste testers if you promise them your daily supply of fresh-baked bread.

Gluten-Free Baking

Gluten-free Artisan Breads Bread can and is made around the world using diverse and wide-ranging grains without any wheat flour and thus no gluten. These breads often look and taste quite different from the wheat-based breads we are accustomed to in the United States, but they have their own singular charm. This mini-section will touch on ways you might be able to modify the breads in this book to bake up gluten-free versions of these recipes. Truth be told, though, these artisan breads, many of which have generous initial flour dustings, are notoriously difficult to do gluten-free. The dough tends to spread and never develops very good structure, making a finished loaf that's kind of flat and homely. This can be very disheartening after you've put the time and effort into baking your loaf only to have it not develop properly.

Gluten-free Flours The only way I've found to bake with gluten-free flours in a bread machine or in the oven is to use special techniques. Unlike with baker's percentages, there is no blanket formula for how you might have to modify your liquid amounts in these recipes. The amount of liquid you will need will vary based on the flour blend you use and conditions like humidity and altitude. For this reason, I also recommend using a flour blend that has the ingredients listed by weight rather than volume on the packaging, such as Bob's Red Mill 1:1 Gluten-Free Baking Flour. When baking gluten-free, all flours are not created equal. A blend will have stabilizers, and the commodity flours have much more protein in them than flour blends that are meant to be an all-in-one mix for lighter baking.

Vegan Baking

Although the vast majority of artisan breads are crafted from animal products, a lot of them can be replicated using vegan ingredients, and this is also true for making artisan bread in the bread machine. A few of the breads covered in this book are actually vegan by using margarine instead of butter, such as Malaysian Coconut Buns, Hawaiian Sweet Bread, and Scandinavian Tea Ring. Several of the basic bread recipes are also vegan as long as you use a sugar not processed through animal charred bones such as Florida Crystals. Also, many of the deli and condiment spreads that melt onto the slices of bread can be made using vegan ingredients.

Most of my recipes listed, which are not vegan, can be vegan by using a commercial egg replacer available at your local grocery store. The egg replacer is good for leavening and adding structure to cakes and breads. It can replace egg yolks in custards and pudding. Because vegan baking is very similar except for the differences in the types of sugar, margarine, and egg replacer, there will be very few vegan recipes shown in this book. Typically, bread that is "vegan" contains no animal products of any kind. For many sweet breads and savory muffins (which are simply quick breads in a loaf shape), sweeten as desired with vegan dried fruit (and powdered/ground dried fruit). You can blend vegan dried fruits with a bit of the recipe's water in a food processor and strain if a chunk-free consistency is desired. Following are a few recipes with vegan ingredients. For a full set of vegan recipes including breads, bagels, rolls, pretzels, pastries, baguettes, elongated rolls, and boules which are shared with the private students at the Colorado Mountain Bakers School.

10

Showcasing Your Artisan Breads

Tips: • Cellophane bags, especially those highly stylized ones with sunflowers or polka dots, work nicely for giving away individual loaves. • Shallow baskets make for an inviting display of a few loaves. • Very inexpensive French bread bags with one large window make for clean and neat presentation of baguettes. • Wooden cutting boards with a loaf of bread and bread knife lying next to it look as if they have been lifted from an illustration of a Modern Country kitchen. • Wrap several small loaves in dish towels and nestle them in a basket.

Ideas: 1. Bake a variety of breads. Giant loaves or "fat boys" and baguettes are particularly beautiful. 2. Family of breads. For example, bake three varieties of English muffins. 3. Create a themed gift. For example, give the gift of French bread from a second recipe rising next to a bottle of wine. Or, pair "meat loaves" with three mustards and a cutting board.

Presentation Tips

Verily, as the old maxim goes, "One cannot live by bread alone." Yet, this does not speak to the joy one derives from the presentation of that daily bread. Artisan bread is lovingly crafted as much by hand as through the methods of any bread machine. In truth, these two methods can procure bread of like quality. Once you encounter the perfection of that warm, crusty loaf from your bread machine, which you masquerade as an artisan creation baked by hand, you will find the presentation makes your gathering more memorable; the bread more delicious to your appreciation and that of your guests. Those guests, who appreciate the experience as eagerly as they do the bread, will be drawn to repeat the event, inspiring you to do the same.

No more should appetizers, dips, butters, snacks, wines or juices bring that appetizing dimension into the light of appreciation at your gatherings. That dimension exists as naturally at your table as does bread. That being said, never serve a loaf of bread with nuts, berries or fruit unless while still warm, as it may be mistaken for a dry or over-baked loaf of bread with anything but yeast. Whole berries of any kind may require you to add additional moisture. When you speak from your heart and tell your family, friends, and guests about the artistic experience of bread making in your home, do not end with briskly serving industrially produced bread as though the time, money, and appreciation you've bestowed on the bread were of necessity and hence secondary at your table. Show, don't tell, the constancy of crafting superior bread at your table and guests will inquire how much you appreciate good company by return invitation.

Gift Ideas

Whether they are made in the bread machine or by hand, these breads are artful and packed with complex flavors. They definitely make delicious gifts. Wrap the breads in clean, new dish towels or red-checkered fabric and attach a card with a recipe for a dish it complements and a packet of herbed butter, a sweet marmalade, a small bottle of flavored oil, or a pretty cheese spreader. Round up those mini sizes for an elegant house-guest gift when visiting. Share your passion and introduce someone new to the wonders of bread with homemade bread mixes. Here's to paying it forward (or, shall I say, paying it flourward?).

- Invest in pint-sized glass Mason jars. - Measure out the dry ingredients for a chosen recipe (or your own proportions) for a bread or pastry recipe, minus the yeast and any perishable or freezable add-ins. Season the flour with a small amount of sea salt. - Layer the dry ingredients in the Mason jar, tapping the heel of the jar firmly on a padded counter, after each ingredient, to make sure the mix compresses tightly. - Attach a plastic baggie with the yeast to the rim of the jar using a rubber band. This is to ensure the yeast stays air- and moisture-tight. - If desired, tuck dried fruits or nuts, paper-wrapped piped pastry fillings, rehydrated molasses figs, oak-aged maple canistos, or petarmel in small treat bags and place in the Mason jar. - Finally, label the jar with a colorful, artistic cardstock. Provide instructions for making the recipe with the other wet ingredients as well as baking directions.

11

Conclusion

I t is hoped that the information contained within this resource has provided you with a better understanding of the world of bread machine mastery and the ease with which you can craft artisan breads that were previously only available from a skilled and specially trained baker. An exploration of wheat kernel structure and composition, gluten and how it is affected by the manner in which the flours are milled, as well as the overall bread making process, as presented, may add to your overall understanding of bread making and provide some background to the formulas and techniques found within this book.

This book seeks to provide you with the procedural techniques and few formulas required for you to be able to effectively use a modern bread machine as if it were a scaled down version of a commercial pan or deck oven. By adding these techniques and proper handling of fermented dough, you will absentmindedly find yourself creating some of the finest breads of your life, at the push of a button and with the touch of a few simple ingredients, something that only a short time ago in the annals of history only the most skilled and dedicated bakers in the world could have accomplished. I hope that the information found in this Ideal Handbook series can serve to guide you down the path of never before realized and surpassed bread perfection. Thank you for allowing me to share this goal with you. Cheers.

Recap of Key Points

The world of artisan breads is vast and old, and more varied than most dare to imagine. Flavor starts when the flour is ground, and its quality is a decision from the farmer. Variations exist not as proportional percentages, but in grams or grams per kilogram. Even a difference of less than 1% can change a flavor profile. Creators can pick up elements from different reference points to craft and influence the final product taste.

The best sandwich breads are based on sourdoughs, even if the breads are ultimately yeast-raised. Enriched sandwich breads begin with a low percentage of preferment, at least 6%. The term "mother" indicates mid-process levains that use either method to refresh them. Their time dialing both flavor and speed, their creation basic and every home baker's starting point to diverse flavors. A formula, offering ingredient weights in grams and in order of their use in the mixing process, comes next, finishing the meat of the writes in 11 pages, describing in meticulous detail both the visual and physical changes to expect during mixing and fermentation. Experimentation – in a second variation on the bread, as well as a scone – and, ultimately, a recipe offer conclusion.

Overnight increases flour's quantity, benefits, and quality. Chorus the gluten in a bread machine throughout mixing, aids in flavor complexity and increase, and produces outstanding results every time. Breads are built on a base of preferment; another name for sourdough that refers to the fact that preferments' starter does just that – it ferments for a while running its starter. Preferments include sourdoughs, bigas, poolishes, levains, mother doughs, and other regional or cultural variations. The key to favorite sandwich breads is found in preferments, essentially. A base sourdough or biga or poolish dough provides each bread's enticing flavor, leap, and texture.

Future of Home Baking

Home bakers have been enjoying the convenience and consistency of electric bread machines for years. Many of those devices were initially clunky yellow boxes. Over the past decade, however, these units have evolved into sleek machines of various sizes, shapes, and colors. One newer model, the T-fal Home Bakery (also sold under the ActiBread label in the United States), offers an approach similar to the Japanese horizontal models introduced in the West. These units have quickly gained popularity.

The future of home baking holds a great deal of potential. In the world of home bread machine mastery, computer processors could be introduced to devices, which would make homemade bread equal to that of professional artisan bakeries. There are also now fully operational models, which make a variety of bread from scratch in a single pan. Some cookbooks have featured these machines with a range of creating different in-store bakery-type rolls and bring a new dimension to the use of high technology in the development of equipment for the home cook.

www.ingramcontent.com/pod-product-compliance
Lightning Source LLC
Chambersburg PA
CBHW030413160726
47992CB00007B/3102